What Is Left of It

What Is Left of It

—— Having Been through It ——

Llaka Tshesane

RESOURCE *Publications* • Eugene, Oregon

WHAT IS LEFT OF IT
Having Been through It

Resource Publications
An Imprint of Wipf and Stock Publishers
199 W. 8th Ave., Suite 3
Eugene, OR 97401

www.wipfandstock.com

PAPERBACK ISBN: 978-1-6667-5765-1
HARDCOVER ISBN: 978-1-6667-5766-8
EBOOK ISBN: 978-1-6667-5767-5

10/12/22

To my loving father, Abram.

I wish you were here to see your little princess manifest into a lady.

The temptations in your life are no different from what others experience. And God is faithful. He will not allow the temptation to be more than you can stand. When you are tempted, He will show you a way out so that you can endure.

—1 Corinthians 10:13

Contents

Preface

I started writing from a very young age, firstly it was only for my healing, to lay my feelings to rest in papers I will later not give thought to. And only after I have written enough from both my personal experiences and emotions only evoked by a wandering mind, have I decided, I will share this part of me with the world.

I want to write a poem

I want to write a poem
with big words and hidden meanings
I want it so perfect it makes my readers cry
I want to write a poem so short it leaves one wanting more
I want it to end on a sad note with a rhetorical question
but I fear for its big words and hidden meanings,
because then my readers won't understand it and thus won't cry
I fear its length will be too short for all my thoughts
so, I have decided to write a simple long poem
fastened with emotions and nicely chosen words

Feet on the ground

Having had no one to talk to

I have written it down

in these pages that won't nod

nor judge me in between their lines

Tell me what I want to hear

or ask questions whose answers are the corners of my life

I'd rather leave unlit

These pages that have allowed me to leave my burden with them,

have kept their end of the bargain

Is it considered good to write instead?

or is it still bottling up bugging matters?

What meets not the eyes

Fitfully what hurts more than an aching heart,

is wearing a fake smile

It is the facade you put on

when all you want is to release the storm swelling within

It is the neglected need to be alone and let go

It is the suppressed desperation to break down

but you hold secure your collapsing inside

and pray the hurt in your eyes isn't speaking over your calculated voice

You hope not to shatter apart in front of these people who will
never understand

And you hold on tighter

Inwardly pleading no one asks you anything further than "how are you?"

Because then you won't be fine anymore

Living in the never

We all have a great desire for acceptance
Should it be our own happiness we snatch
or our comfort we neglect
Long as he acknowledges your presence
and she approves of your accomplishments
But within the comfort of our dorms
where we have no soul to impress
This happiness we so desperately seek, finds us not
and it is then we realise at the foot of death
That we have not lived

Unravel

I've broken down in the shower

I've sealed my facade to hide my cracks

I've smiled to shelter my sorrows

And swallowed my point of view

But never once had my eyes lied,

Never once had they been selfish enough not to show my true emotions

Blues

Some days are easier

I walk through them like I am one of a kind

Other days are not

and I cannot leave my bed

Some nights are beautiful, others are not

The medicines on my nightstand,

I have taken enough to rely on

and I need one more to knock me unconscious

Some hot days I still pull the covers over my head

and leave my curtains unopened,

Because it is bright out unlike my within

and it makes me unsettled

Today is one of those days

When I cannot leave my bed

nor open my curtains

Because they are here

Serenity

I hope to wake up one night,

To cut sleep short for a peace I want to cherish

To wake up in the arms of my lover

and smile at our tangled limbs and their drooling mouth

I wish to be sleepless,

only this time for a happy reason

not a nightmare

Afore the storm

When morning comes and you open your eyes

I wish you'd smile,

from the peace your vacant mind provides

I pray you would appreciate the sunrays coming through your windows

Acclaim the 2 seconds of the void paradise

The soothing sound by the clock on the wall

The stillness besides that, decontaminating the atmosphere

I hope you relish it all before the abrupt heartache

The pinching feeling delivered in your ribcage and the sudden replay of the past day's reminiscences

Because then you would long for its occurrence

You would wish to have cherished the temporary amnesia when it was offered

To busk in its presence and never feel the pain that comes after

The infuriating noises the clock shall make

and the now unwelcomed sunrays gifting an annoyingly blinding light

Prompting you of a new day already full of timeworn memories

Oh, how merciless yesterday is to make you live through its torture again

Doom's Day

Thy doom shall cometh
though thee quickens to hide
If that be,
thy end shall shadow thee there
for thy please gearshifts not the clock
nor thy prayers alter thy doom
thou no god to front thy death
though thee run up to the highland top
or sneak beneath the deep's feet
though thee seek refuge in food
or living quarters sniffing all good
thee shall breathe no more,
when thy doom has arisen
At the nature's 6th feet
thy figure shall depart its existence,
and thee shall live no more

Dear Dad

I hate on the world for what it has done to you
the pieces of lungs the cigarettes have stolen from you
the alcohol that fed on you,
and the stroke that snatched your life too
I hate the loss mama goes through
the sight of her puffy red eyes every morning
and sounds of fought cries every night
although it is good that you rest in peace
it is far from okay to live in your absence
to wake up to no candy on my nightstand
nor money under my pillow
If heavens allowed letters, you would have been the most receiver
I would have liked to say goodbye
now that I know you cannot return to me

Catch-22

Oh, how cold the trail of your existence must be

Your memories painfully unacknowledged,

Your photos still hung up with the rest on the wall

It's saddening that no one stops for them anymore

You have become a sensitive topic

No one dares to say your name

No one brings up your sturdily selfless kind heart

Your absence is very flashy, it's hard to miss

And the sympathetic looks stolen my way,

Reminds me why I never needed a friend when I had you

It upsets me that you aren't holding my hand anymore

This woman you've taught me to become

You aren't watching her manifest

the guilt of your fading face feeds off me

and I only look like you in my actions

the reflection starring back in the mirror it is still that innocent child
hoping for your return

Unspoken fears

The thoughts sneak in slowly
From how you've lost a parent, to how you are only left with one.
They wander to the hidden spots
To the avoided sensitive topic
To the unspoken fears,
of waking up to a crying brother or a broken sister
The questions thoroughly marching through the head are a lot
So much it feels wrong to ask any of them
The guilt of already knowing the answer
The fear that you might be right
"I am sorry, we did everything we could. . ."
The doctor would say,
and you would break before the end of that sentence
For there was no smile in his eyes
There was no "okay" in that phrase
Then it would creep in,
how you are of no parents
"It's all my fault . . ."—you conclude
"I should have . . ."—you add
Before later, you realise these are all just wandering curiosities
Imaginations you decide to bury deep down
Afraid if you tell them to another,
they might become reality

Guns Down

In a fantasy that lasted a minute
I fell for the peace there would have been
Had we learnt to love one another
And not shied from the freedom of just being
No walls shielding our hearts
No disguise detaining our emotions
Had we respected the man expressing his feelings
And thanked the lady giving wholeheartedly
Had we freely been,
without fear of betrayal
nor that of judgement
If we had loved our neighbour as we do ourselves
Maybe it would not have been just a fantasy

A date with destiny?

Beyond that mask you wear so well
Behind those walls you hide determined
I bet you are only human
You are enough for this woman having mutual feelings
and returning them openly makes you no less of a man
If anything, it makes you human
For does every Adam not need his Eve?
Defeat your snakes together

Fatum nos iungebit

Fate will unite us

I have seen it in the movies
I have read it in the books
The healing of the broken heart
And the finding of new love
As I wait for my own
I pray to the good Lord I serve
That it is the ending I yearn for

Dear soulmate

I have thought of you

I have planned our future,

and the memories we will make

I have revised our first fight

and who will be wrong

I have decided to start loving you

So much that should you break me,

I would let you

I have given thought to our vows

How mushy I will be when saying mine

I have thought about how romantic it will all be,

I might end up crying

I thought about our honeymoon too

About the rest of our lives and I am pleased

I have thus concluded that I miss you,

And that I cannot wait to meet you

If I am honest

I want love so perfect I smile in my sleep
I want it with a man who will make it home for dinner,
and not confuse romance for a bullet to his manhood
Though I want him rough around the edges and nothing near perfect
I want him free and happy
I want our children to look up to him
without being sickened by his tendency
to drown his liver in alcohol
nor flaming his lungs black in the name of fun
I want them worry-free of the possibilities:
That daddy might die from drug abuse
To live not in fear of being down to a single parent
I want them free and happy
I want to be free and happy

Perfect storm

I want to leave a mark
without breaking your heart
I want to get intimate
without sexual intercourse
I want to know your state
without a verbal confession
I want to sleep next to you
with intentions just so
I want not to ask
when you can willingly give
I want this and that
But you want them

The tip of the iceberg

Happiness and blushing

Daydreaming and imaginations,

Romantic images

Dinner and a walk around the park,

time off from everything but one you are with

Late chats and long phone calls,

a yearn for each other's presence

Disappointment and tears,

an agony by whom you never expected

Tight hugs and forehead kisses,

an appreciation from a close friend

Nudes and saliva exchange,

the fruits of lust

Flowers and song dedications,

a revelation of significance

Love is an ambiguous word to cite

and it would be foolish to use it for the overhead

Babe in the woods

In the movies,

the happiness after the loss

the smiles after that tearing agony

the clingy get together scenes

You envy for your own,

for your turn,

your get together

But it feels as if you are missing a step

The lurking void does not go away

It does not help that you buried your ability to wait

You long for the love you could have

You thirst for your own,

so much you settle for anything glancing your way

And you stay, with that being who wants everything but you

Long as you are not single?

Get up and leave!

Deep down

In your reality,
You have never been another's priority
And that has made you become
To smile and laugh with the willing
To be there for the one needing a hand
After the event,
You have returned to your corner alone,
to be with you
Because only you have valued you openly,
Only you have allowed your intimacy to be

So far not good

In the cold darkening bedroom

She hugged her legs, miserably waiting for Paul

He had gone out to the mall

And she knew not to call

How happy they seem in that photo across the hall

Outside, it is already nightfall

If it was back then, she would have cried

Down in the basement

She finds a picture of her ex-lover, Clyde

It is one thing she forgot to hide

It brought back memories she never quashes

When she hears Paul's ride

Quickly she puts the picture back in the box

"I was on the phone with an old friend"

She lied

Turn back time

If I could turn back the clock
and face that hour I have missed
Do all the things I left out of the list,
like buying you a lot of gifts
and getting every silly thing I did fixed
Remember not to get you tea with milk mixed
Wet your lips of my kisses
Be that girl you constantly sought
The one whose heart you tirelessly desired
I am unhappy,
Your absence—enfolding me dry
I lament,
for the love I could not bury
and you whom I could not with carry

Love

I am happy to have had you

I am glad I experienced you

To feel you in his opinions when he spoke

And see you in his eyes each gaze

When you made me weep at the declaration of his no longer

I feared I had lost you with

That uninterrupted pain with a striking mark

I had feared it will remain just so,

and I would desire your company more than his

How more self-centred could I have been?

Fair share

She is on a path,

many had already left their footprints on

She leaves her own trail

Stepping at her own pace,

Healing at her particular rate

Why rush her?

When she will get there when she does

When she has had her time to heal

When her wounds have turned into artless scars

How she lost it

You drew her in,

offering her weakness

You have smiled at your vile thoughts

The possibility of your actions brought you zest

Ripping her of her pride relieved your tension

Her unease brought you to your high,

it rode your waves

and it does not alarm you, her broken trust

You smile at the sight of her

like only you know what most do not

Maybe that is true

Maybe she had not told

Why she really grew out this way

Confined in her space by herself

Why the reflection in the mirror is always lacking,

and the guy showing genuine interest still does not stand a chance

Why she goes through her days like someone driving through a fog:

Tormentingly slow,

Careful,

Enjoying nothing!

Scars

To have or not to have

To walk or to sit

To stand and take the hits

To hide from the war ahead

These decisions I have not carried

These diverging roads that have left me double-edged

I have sat at their intersection,

and waited for fate that was never on my side

Now I am plumped into its coughed up

and it is everything I know I would have aimed above

if only I had decided

Been there, Done that

To be left behind,

To watch these flowers I gardened,

blossom quicker than my future

It is torture

To lose one who is not dead

To watch them walk away like I meant nothing

The sacrifices I make to have them stay

To not have to watch them leave

The fear of feeling lonely

Failure to see real fear should be losing myself

But these toxic relationships I keep require me to be anything but myself

Meet death

To give to these people who keep taking

To accept apologies never received

And say thank you to their unusable "I don't know"

It is an unsettling closure

To provide calmness despite your inside war

To offer to another what you need the most

To make excuses why they are the way they are

To pretend not to care that things are so

Your once joyful remembrances are hard to leave behind

Though it is harder to stay

They apologise to ease their guilt,

the self-seeking has not stopped

Why have you not cut loose?

Reality check

On the other end of the relation
I know you are busy
And your mind is reeling with everything but me
That is the sad truth
That is reality

Descendants of Judas

At the bottom of the ocean,

It is the survival of the fittest

The creatures see a new dawn by snatching another's

In your head, is no different

The lies feed off your sanity

They survive by speaking louder than the rest

And are hard not to listen to,

when they are all you can hear

They destroy you ever so slowly,

And you hope you do not die before you have become

Late night discoveries

These attractive blank pages of my diary lure me in
I have more than enough to fill them with
But these lines looking back at me
This attractive blankness begging me to leave it so
Reminds me of you
Of your attractive emptiness
There is no filling between your lines
No life amid your pages
You have nothing to offer but beauty

But you keep taking

I have sat under a tree for its shade
I have eaten its fruits and gave my water
We have shared the sun's company
and gave our excretions
But you keep taking
From the meaning of this band on my finger
To the heart I no longer wear up my sleeves
They share and care better,
these trees that are incapable of love
are more human than you

Cheating is a verb

To have a man driven by skirts
To have his zips controlled
But not by you
He fathers many fatherless
But who wants to be the mistake from a deliberate act?
Or one of the many skirts now thrown in the basket?

An endless fall

Pain
It spreads across my tightening chest
It hurts,
and I am only solid enough to gasp in the yells
Tears had already achieved their practice out
The reflection in the mirror starring back,
reveals scars that feed my self-doubt
Like a punch in the gut,
it reminds me of the flaws making me imperfect
it urges more tears that blur my vision
and for a second, I believe- this is it:
Rock bottom
But you pull another stunt
And I discover it wasn't

Maybe ignorance is bliss

Behind closed doors lies uncertainty
There be one who is at rest,
having a nightmare or being the best
In there awaits a method to separation
for in there occurs actions strong enough to ruin marriage
Behind closed doors,
I hear voices from faces I cannot see
they whisper what they want unknown,
and giggle at there on an inside joke
When the doors finally open,
everything is on the spot like a park
And most things leave a mark

Not a hallmark moment

Occasionally I contemplate my existence

The present

And for a moment everything seems stable

Promising?

But I am still tumbling in storms and my heart is heavy on darkness

Then I remember: that's my plain

Hullabaloo

Cognitively wrestling for a new dawn is my portion

In a nutshell

I know the back of your hand more than my own
I am familiar with its cruel knuckles
The middle one hurts more
Not more than the belt, but it hurts
And not more than the kicks, but it hurts
It hurts more than the words
Though their pain stays the longest
They echo in my head all night
And haunt my thoughts in day light
They remind me every time: I am not enough
They talk me to the edge of my era
Right where you are, waiting
For something, anything to go south
To relieve yourself
Someday, I hope, you relieve me too

Lord it over

Smile,

You did it!

You came out on the other end,

not without scars, but you did it

Mid-way when you thought it would be the end of you

You were there to carry yourself one more step

It was all you,

You did it!

Come rain or shine

Off the time I will never regain

I don't live it gloomily arranging a past I cannot change

Or living in paths I'll never take

I spend it planning my future

Highlighting consequences of actions I never want to repeat

I will say

I am my pillar of strength

I've been the one keeping me from coming undone

I was the little voice that spoke over the negative thoughts

I kept me sane

I am the patient one who didn't give up on me

I had my back

When I fell, I picked me up

Keep the peace

Take a deep breath in, hold it

Take a deep breath out

Repeat

Do that with all that shakes your faith in the impending

And everything that changes your mood for the worst

Damn straight

Sinking in the presence of my anxiety
I have listened to it talk me into not reaching my potential
I smiled at it after an event I left too soon
and I lied to myself that the silence behind my doors never gets too loud,
that I am good and just a loner
I have said it too long to know when it is all a lie
though I enjoy my own company
and I'd rather be alone than under the lenses of judgemental minds
I am still not always happy
and sometimes I need more company than I could provide for myself
I need company when the silence gets too loud

Safe and sound

I hide behind these words I unfold

Editing these thoughts that swim within me

I am their creator and them equally my maker

I am a product of their survival

They are a result of my openness

We have become one

Our intimacy is untainted

And so is our love

It carries no inequality,

No tradition

Pull yourself together

Raging winds are a melody to nature enthusiasts,
a threat to the underweight
To whiners it is an addition to the list
To the one cleaning,
it is more or less work out the yard
When this one occurrence is beheld inversely by the mass
How come you want to be perceived the same by everyone?

Red

Red: Love or Danger?

How dare one colour be so self-contradictory

Prompting a woman to love a stranger

And have a man feel endangered

I guess it makes sense after all:

It all ends the opposite way it has started

A good deal

Past midnight,
I am all but asleep
Thinking, concluding
I have been through it all
Haven't I?
Like a soldier returning from war
I am not elegantly wounded
There are parts of me I had to leave behind,
to survive
Given a chance, I'd do it the same again
Just to become

What is left of it

Having lived through it
I can finally say, I am stronger than I'd thought
Since you haven't been through it,
You don't get to decide
If I should have healed by now

In seventh heaven

I have been lonely in a company of another
I have laughed at a joke I didn't understand
Danced to a song whose lyrics I couldn't relate to
I reasoned that something was deficient in me,
That I had to give it sometime
But with you it's effortless, graceful
I bask into our calm silence
Smiling at the stillness it offers
No need to fill it with sound,
It is complete
Raw
I realize only upon my waking that I had dozed
It's peaceful what we have,
It's surreal

Life of a colouring book

If only life was a like a colouring book
Then I'd choose which page to start with,
and leave it undone when I get bored
I'd skip to another page, and another after that
As the page becomes unsatisfactory
I'd tear it out and forget of its existence
It would be nice to shade the feelings I want
If my day should be bright or gloomy
I would colour outside the margins too, outside what's projected on me
I'd decide the shade of my monsters, I'd see them coming
Should they scare me despite, I'd page through and forget them
When the book is full, and I'd coloured all my pages
I'd grab another one and never die